GROWTH SPRINT IN 21 DAYS

DAILY DEVOTIONAL

By *KATHERINE MOORING-RUFFIN*

Printed in the United States of America

ISBN: 978-0-9912854-0-2

Table of Contents

ACKNOWLEDGEMENTS

This book is dedicated to my children, Sonya and Benjamin. It is my desire to see them, as well as you, to move from where you are now to a deeper and better place in Christ through faith in and by Him. The greatest knowledge of all is to know for yourself that He will help you. I want to say thanks to Ben, and especially Sonya for being there to read, answer questions, and make suggestions.

Also, it is in memory of my sister Delores, deceased in 2006, who love the bald eagle, the Lord Jesus Christ, and she loved to travel.

I know what it is like to be in a place that appears not to be moving as if the whole world has a hold on you, and it just will not allow you to move, NO MATTER HOW HARD YOU TRY.

Remember, nothing remains the same, something has to happen. It is my hope that all who read this book will move upward in life in a more powerful way. I know it can happen for you.

A final thanks to the publishers, family members, and all of you that will purchase and read this book. Again, Thanks to all!

PURPOSE/VISION

The intent of this devotional book is to show you how to enhance your growth in the Lord. Also, to instruct you in an interactive way that will defeat the pitfalls and downfalls in life that you may be facing or will face. Keep in mind that no one stays down forever. Every dark cloud gives way to the sunshine in time. Therefore, no matter how hard or rough times get, some release has to come. Yes, a change has to take place whether it is physical or mental, but a **CHANGE.**

Isaiah 54:17	*No weapon formed will prosper*

This book is also designed to cause you to study, to practice being in the presence of the Lord, to be conscious of who you are, and to be aware of the greatness within you. Your relationship will be enhanced as you meet the Lord daily.

You will notice for each day there is no set format or ritual, which will allow the Holy Spirit room to have its way. The only items that remain consistent are the daily scriptures and the write commands. You are to read the daily scriptures, and each day record notes with place, date, and time. The dates are keys in pointing out special times that something may occur. For instance, two years later you could reread your notes and on that day at that time something may have happened that could have jarred your memory. To journalize is your responsibility daily in conjunction with what else come to your mind to do.

Memory is increased with repetition especially when it occurs 3 or more times. To find the chapter, read the verses, and repeat them several times is to help grind you in the word, and for you to get to know more about the God of the Heavens and the Earth through His Word. Without a vision for your life, your way will be null and void. Catch hold of the word for it will lighten your path.

It is my hope that the VISION of this book will become habitual in your life and turn you on to *The Comforter*, your helper.

My prayer for you…..

Lord, help each reader to catch the vision that you have for their lives and use it as a keepsake. Teach them all to hear you. Give a double blessing to each and every person that reads this book. Thank you! In Jesus' name! Amen.

Author, KMR

HOW TO GET THE MOST OUT OF THIS BOOK

It is important that you designate a place and time that will be convenient, and that can be available for the next 21 days.

There is a section devoted to each day with important points to follow. Keep this in mind as you read and interact with these messages that are inside. It is imperative that each person that reads this book be him/herself, that is, being genuine and the rest will take care of itself. Some people may have to read this book from cover to cover several times before they can commit to the message of helping yourself and taking the challenge of this **Growth Sprint in 21 Days.**

So start your day as you always do, whatever that is, some may read, pray, listen to music, or just get up and start moving without saying anything.

However it is a good thing to **Thank the Lord** for the day, and ask Him to bless your way.

As you get started, I am sure that you will find that this book will be very helpful, useful, and can be used and appreciated by all ages and people from all walks of life. This daily devotional will help to tailor your life style. There was a time in my life when I needed my life tailored, and I am glad that it happened in time and not too late.

Be sure that you read the section for each day just before the actual timing to familiarize yourself with what you are to do that day. Have your notepad and pencil with you to take the appropriate notes as you see or hear them. Suppose you feel that a day needs to be repeated, then repeat that day, in other words don't move to the next day until you feel comfortable.

It is equally imperative that you have time to spend building up your **Faith**, and <u>DO NOT</u> come to this place in a hurry and not have enough time, because the time that you may have set to leave could just be when there is going to be a move of the Spirit. You do not want to miss this moment. Keep in mind that a moment missed cannot be retrieved by you or me. **Only God can redeem the times** as you yield yourself to Him. Many of you know that when this day is over it is over, and you cannot call it back into existence. All you can do at that point is start on the next day which will be a perpetual motion of missed events with the Spirit of the Lord if you are not careful and do not allow precious time to go wasted.

Reminder, the Lord will be there each and every time whether you are there or not. As a matter of fact He will be there waiting on you when you get there, that is how much He wants to be with you. Guess what, when you are late don't worry; He will be there; however, I would not allow late to be in the way. Let me share with you what I see when someone is **late chronically**: someone not reliable, dependable, cannot be trusted, and certainly not loyal to the cause. No one wants to associate with anyone that is always late or in a hurry. Now you know that things happen once and a while beyond your control, God is wise enough to know the difference. Remember **He is God**. If a time is set between you and Him, try to keep it. Even dealing with people in general, be honest; if you agree to something and cannot make it happen, get back with the person as soon as possible to make the necessary changes.

Change the date, time, place, or whatever it takes to show a level of **integrity.**

Remember the Lord will be waiting on you. <u>Each</u> <u>day</u> go to your <u>designated place</u> on the <u>time</u> that <u>you</u> <u>set</u> and stay there until that time has expired.

NOTE OF ENCOURAGEMENT

I have personally followed the instructions in this book, and I am still amazed at the blessings that I have reaped from being obedient to the Word, and the message that are shared between these pages. This book was truly God inspired from beginning to end. Its format can be easily altered and adaptable to meet the needs of your particular situation.

Moreover, the time or day can be changed to a week or even a month. For instance, if you have a certain fault that lingers or you cannot seem to shake it; you may need more than one day; in case of this issue, a week may be needed, allow the Spirit to direct and instruct you. That is the primary mission of this devotional; to ultimately allow you an avenue to know that the Lord will and can be supreme in your life, and that you can trust Him. The power of the Lord is incredible.

So if you repeat a day, miss a day, rearrange a day, or a one-day experience is carried over to a week, Thank God and just do it His Way; *He is the way (John 14:6).* There is a counter on page 52 to help you keep track. Moreover, you just might want to check out the whole book before you start the challenge to see the format and get helpful hints to assist in being successful.

My advice is to start off each day with prayer. Make sure that your prayers are not one-sided; "I need or I want", but a mixture of requests including praying for others and thanking the Lord of His goodness. The fervent prayer or most effective prayer is when the Holy Ghost prays through you, and you are not aware of what He is saying—that heavenly language is speaking in other tongues. (Isaiah 28: 11) Ask for it during this **Growth Sprint.**

THE ORDER: Pace Yourself

Read the scriptures for each day on that day.

Read the scriptures 3 to 5 times and meditate on them. Be sure you get your Bible, find each scripture, and read it from your favorite version of the Bible. The shared boxed scriptures are written in part, not the entire verse.
The purpose here is to indirectly study the Word of God, and learn where various books are located in the Bible along with how they are spelled; you will not see any abbreviations in this devotional.

Read what is to be done on a certain day and follow what you are led to do in conjunction with what you have read. The rest will be up to you and the Lord.

Take the time to **WRITE** any comments, scriptures, phrases, songs, etc that comes to your thoughts after the session is over. If you cannot write it down right away, be sure to write as soon as possible. There are extra note pages inserted at the back of this book.

As you work in this daily devotional you will see a visual change in your life and others will too. If tears flow on any given day that's okay; because no one is in this place except you, and the one that can make a difference in your life. Allow Him to bless YOU AS ONLY HE CAN. Take care and pride in selecting an appropriate time to start this challenge, the earlier the time the more you can meditate on the scriptures that day, as opposed to a later time or even bedtime. However, whatever is best for you, I know the Lord will make it work for you.

ARE YOU READY FOR THE CHALLENGE?

Let's get started. Did you notice that I did not say anything about knowing Christ? You know why? Everyone needs Christ in their lives whether they believe that or not. This book is designed to get you from where you are to where you need to be in Him with practice and faith in what He will do for you. Do not become complacent in your faith. Allow your measure of faith to come alive, and help you to be all you can become and do all you can do.

YOU ASK-- HOW CAN I HELP MYSELF?

CALL ON GOD? Can anyone call on God? YES!! You call out of a pure heart. I know because, I had to call on Him one day. He answered me and delivered me. He will do the same for you; He has no respect of persons.

As you read the daily scriptures over and over, you will find that they will become a part of your spirit which will allow you to meditate on the scriptures through the day no matter where you go.

Romans 10:13	*Whosoever call* ...

Keep your notepad and pencil handy. Pick a place that is convenient and that you can possibly visit for the next 21 days. Location is key, as well as time of day, all need to be the same from day 1 to day 21 with the date. If you have to improvise that is okay.

A Song of Praise for the LORD's Faithfulness to His People. A Psalm of Thanksgiving.

Make a joyful shout to the LORD, all
You lands!
Serve the LORD with gladness;
Come before His presence with
Singing.

Know that the LORD, HE IS God;
It is He who has made us, and not we
Ourselves;
We are His people and the sheep of
His pasture.

Enter into His gates with
Thanksgiving,
And into His courts with **praise.**
Be thankful to Him, and bless His
name.

For the LORD is good;
His mercy is everlasting,
And His truth endures to all generations.

PSALMS 100 - NEW SPIRIT FILLED LIFE Bible NKJV

LET THE CHALLENGE BEGIN!

DAY 1 – Introductory Day

Call on the name of the Lord and believe that He hears you. Open your mouth and say J-E-S-U-S! I know some of you have never come before the Lord in this manner. That is okay! Now that you have called Him; you have His attention, and He has yours. Tell Him who you are, and that you will come to this place for the next 21 days, at the same time; also, tell Him how long you will stay there. Make friends with Him, and tell Him anything you want Him to know about yourself. Thank Him and Listen! To make the most of this day, don't be in a **HURRY**, make sure that you can afford to spend quality time with the Lord. NO **ONE KNOWS HOW LONG OR WHEN HE WILL RESPOND.** Don't **DOUBT** in your heart that He will hear you. You must believe. Don't be surrounded by **DISTRACTIONS** of any kind. Allow this to be just God and you.

Whatever happens today is good, you did something different. You are expecting Him to answer you. You may not hear an audible voice, instead you may sense something in your heart, but you cannot rule out anything. Therefore, a very quiet atmosphere is the norm, and I know that some of you have not experienced this. If your house and day is like most it is very busy and noisy.

Tell yourself, **"God hears me."** **Read aloud the daily scripture**.

Psalms 4:1, 3   *The Lord will hear when I call...*

Note-taking is a key at this point to keep tabs on the mysteries that will be unlocked. Don't be surprised if you get entrepreneur insight and much more before this time is up or the next 19 days are over. Don't forget to **write** everything that comes to mind after this session has ended. Also, mark an **X** over #1 on the counter, page 52, if you are not going to repeat the activity for this day. Allow the counter to aid in keeping track of days covered and where to start.

Katherine Mooring-Ruffin

NOTES:

DAY 2 – Thank the Lord

Thank the Lord for whatever happened the day before. Be sure you say exactly what it was that you recognized that happened. Example: supposed that you spent 30 minutes and there was a peace like you have never felt before or a quietness that you had never experienced before. **THANK GOD FOR IT**!

Everyone says "thank you" after an act of kindness from another human, how much more should we thank the Lord for spending time with us and giving us witty ideas. Remember, if Jesus had to thank God, how much more should you thank Him? Another time with the Lord is almost over, the **GROWTH SPRINT** is on. Run for your prize!

This day may become emotional, so be sensitive. Do not try to stop any feelings or emotions that may come at this time. Also, you may feel like you cannot stop Thanking Him, and you cannot. That is why your life has to be lived in such a way that it says **Thank You!** However, you can leave this place silently thanking the Lord all day, no one will know – just you and Him. What a blessing!

Read aloud the scripture.

John 11:41	*Father, I thank you*.

Write down any thoughts or comments that come to you when you have spent the appointed time in the presence of the Lord. Write and revisit your script at a later time each day.

Notes:

DAY 3 – Great, we are getting some place!

Now depending on where your **walk is in Christ**, you will be ready to move on task with day 3, or you may feel like you need to repeat days 1 and 2. By now you should be feeling a real connection with Jesus, and you are looking forward to being with Him. If you do not feel a connection, you may want to repeat the first two days, in essence start all over again. He, on-the-other-hand, wants to be with you. This is NOT a one-sided act. **Will He Save you or Deliver you? YES, He will.**

Moving forward in day 3. Ask the Lord to direct **your FOOT- STEPS**, because that is exactly what He says He will do for those that love Him and follow His commands. On this day stay before the Lord, long enough, until you know that you are not doing your own thing. It is like forgetting everything that you thought that you would do for a moment. You cannot remember anything that you thought that you were going to do the next few minutes. YES! **No thoughts of your own**. You want **instructions** and **directions** on this day from Jesus; therefore, you cannot do all the talking, say what you want to say to Him and **BE SILENT**. You cannot talk while God is speaking, no matter what you are saying. **It will be a great day!**

Read aloud the scripture. Ask Him to order your footsteps. Tell Him that you are waiting for your directions and instructions now; then thank Him, and be quiet.

Psalms 119:133	*Order my steps in your word.*

Make notes of your God given thoughts and comments that will come to you when the appointed time has expired.

Notes:

DAY 4 – CAST OFF YOUR CARES

By now you are getting use to coming to this place at the appointed time to meet the Lord, and He now knows that you will be before Him. Why? This has been an ongoing, consistent, on point, and same place rendezvous.

This is a great day to **Cast your cares** on the Lord and leave them there with Him. How do you do that? I am glad you asked. It is kind of like 'show and tell' except this time you are talking to the Lord Jesus Christ. Remember He is listening. We believe that. So now trust Him to handle it, by refusing *to worry* or *be weary* over issues in your life. Yes, actively tell yourself "**I am not going to think about this or entertain it in my thoughts**." Say "**Lord, please help me to give this issue to you TODAY**". It does not matter what the problem is—simply stated, if you could have fixed the problem you would have. Remember a THING is only a problem or dilemma in life, because the person <u>cannot</u> fix or <u>change</u> it for neither that moment nor forever, and need help.

Read aloud the scripture. Just give everything to Jesus and believe He can fix it or handle it, and He WILL. Give Him thanks!

1 Peter 5:6, 7, 10   *Cast all your cares upon Him.*

Write down anything that comes to mind such as comments, scriptures including the date, time and place of these God given ideas and comments.

Notes:

DAY 5 – A time of intimacy

Come to this special place at the appropriate time and do not **ask for anything** or **say anything**. Just sit, stand, bow down before Him, or lay prostrate in whatever position you feel comfortable in the presence of the Lord. This challenge may be harder than the previous days, because the interruptions may be bolder, like phone ringing, door bell ringing, clock ticks even the washing machine noise, sounds inside and outside the house like car horns, train, planes, or anything to disturb. Blot them all out. Don't give in or be interrupted during this special appointed time, you will find your breakthrough on the other side of this wait.

The aftermath of this day will show you just how strong your will and mind is to do what you want, and not be completely silent especially mentally; which implies talking but not speaking out loud. (The mind has a tendency to wonder and do its own agenda.)

Remember, **you are not talking or asking for anything, but** concentrating on the daily scripture. God is able to search your heart, and know what is in it. Trust the Lord whole- heartedly. In your silence you are speaking very loudly to the sound of '**show me your love and your glory, Lord Jesus Christ.**'

Read aloud the scripture, it should be repeated 3-5 times or more. Thank Him and be silent.

Zechariah 2:13	*Be silent, all flesh before the Lord.*

When the time is up, get up, and say or **write** what you felt along with your God given thoughts and comments as you have done in the past. Thank Him for helping you to write each day. You may leave any time that the writing session has ended, if you have to leave before you write remember to resume writing as soon as possible.

Notes:

DAY 6 – Praise the Lord

For the progress that He has helped you to make so far, It's not quite the same as giving thanks to the Lord. To praise Him is to think on and speak on his goodness and all that He is about to you. To praise the Lord is to concentrate more on what he really means to you. On the other hand, to thank the Lord is more about giving homage about what He has done for you. Someone can **'THANK THE LORD'** and **still not PRAISE HIM, but it is impossible to Praise the Lord without thanking Him.** In the praise the one praising has to first thank God for giving him the mind to praise. Once that thanks is out and good – move into telling the Lord just what He means to you and how marvelous He is. Praise is all about lifting Him up.

One of the greatest tools that you and I can use or possess is a life of praise. It is one thing to praise the Lord Jesus with our lips of clay and it is another thing to live your life as praise unto Him.

Living a life of praise is to do the right thing at all times. Do not deliberately set out any day to do something that you know is wrong. Be mindful that someone is watching you; they just may be the little eyes that are the closest to you or other acquaintances.

Read aloud the scripture.

Psalms 150	***Let all that are breathing praise the Lord.***

Praise with your mouth: "Lord I love you, and I thank you, Lord you are wonderful, you are mighty, you are great, without you I can do nothing nor can I be anything in the earth that can make a real difference in the lives of others. Glory to your name Lord for your forgiving power, grace, righteousness, mercy, and......."

Write down any God given thoughts, comments, scriptures, etc be sure to record the date, time, and place of each event with the Lord.

Notes:

DAY 7 -- HAVE FAITH

If you have gotten this far you are serious and so is God. God has been serious from day 1. Today put your **FAITH IN HIM**. There will come a time in life when you will have to have all hope and trust in the Lord. You will have to do this whether you can see it or not. Why not start right now; you must put all your hope and faith in the Lord. This is not just for one or two days, but you are to do this as a way of life. Remember, **when all else fail try Jesus! He will come to the rescue**. If there is something going on or perhaps you need a raise on the job or even a new job or any number of things; I say to you HAVE **FAITH IN GOD**. You must have faith in the one that speaks from heaven. He has the power to speak a thing into existence. Believe God! **HE WILL SEE YOU THROUGH. HE IS FAITHFUL.**

Today read Hebrews 11:1 and mediate on that scripture. Ponder over it and envision having just what it is that you need. If time permits read the entire chapter in this text. When you leave this place, put your faith in that word to work, **BELIEVE** even though you cannot see anything happening for the moment. Ask Him to increase your **FAITH** and thank Him.

You can depend on the Lord; He is the God that keeps his promises. Trust Him with all your heart in full confidence.

Hebrews 11:1	*Now Faith is...*

Write down any scriptures, words, phrases, comments, draw a picture, or whatever comes to your mind. Date it and review your notes daily. Do not forget about the counter on page 52; x-out.

Notes:

DAY 8 – RENEW MY MIND LORD

It takes a changed mindset to move from one place to another as far as living is concerned. Let's face it, if you continue to think like you do right now, you will continue to do the things that you are doing now. Those doings that you are displaying may be good or bad, right or wrong, without a changed mind this will continue to happen. Do we agree? However, on the other hand with a **CHANGED MIND**, you will do a new thing with your life and living in general. For instance, friends may change, jobs may change, you will not be the same, but most of all you will change in the way you perceive situations. Things that use to hurt you or move you will not be able to do so as easily. What a great way—nothing can bless better than being able to <u>NOT be affected by the things you</u> <u>hear,</u> <u>see,</u> or <u>feel</u>, because you have been CHANGED in your mind. Old things will not move you like they use to and you will have a different walk and talk. Let's thank the Lord right here right now. Go on! **Also ask Him to give you a new mind; then you do not act on negative thoughts or actions anymore, because you will be able to recognize them and respond in a positive manner**.

Read aloud, ask, and receive.

Ephesians 4:22-24	*Be renewed in the spirit of you mind.*

Write down all words, comments, scriptures, or even vividly describe whatsoever you see before leaving this place. Be sure to affix the date, time, and place each time your notes are written.

Notes:

DAY 9 – Pray and spend time listening

This is a wonderful day, let us pray that nothing hinders the way we feel or what good is due to come to us.

Everyone can pray, because all of us pray especially when something goes wrong or is very traumatic in our lives. We pray!

Prayer is simply talking to God about issues in life, which includes presenting to Him the cares of life, pains of all kind, wants, needs, and/or desires. There are several types of prayer, which I will not go in depth at this time, but I will say, as you allow the Spirit of the Lord to pray through you, you will pray the fervent prayer. **Just ask God to HELP you to pray in Jesus' name, open your mouth, and speak.** Don't think about what you are saying, just trust that The Lord will give you the right words to say. Prayer is two-way communication, which is a conversation between you and the Lord. However you should listen more than you speak. It is important to hear God once you end your complaints or request.

Read aloud, ask, and receive.

Go on and try it now! When you run out of words, **STOP** then **LISTEN** intently to hear a word from the Lord. You may sense a moving or auction from His Spirit, which is inside of you; acknowledge it.

Luke 11:1-4	*Lord, teach us to pray*

Write down any comments, thoughts, or patterns of things you notice NOW and throughout the day. Write them with the time, date, and place inscribed in your notes.

Notes:

DAY 10 – BE SINCERE

Integrity is very important to God. Make sure that each and everything you do today, you consider the fact that we represent the Lord. **BE HONEST**!

In the presence of the Lord, don't hide anything; just let God know about everything. Yes! Those backroom, behind the scene vices are included. Remember He is omnipresent and He knows all things, therefore, He is already aware of your hang-ups and short comings.

While you **SEEK THE LORD today**, you can stand assured of the grace and mercy of Christ. I know how it is when one is not honest. It is not a good feeling, been there done that. Also, I have had folks tell me that they felt like someone was looking right through them or that they had to work harder to keep their faults covered up. However, if they had told it or made it known, then they would have been done with the situation. In other words, one bad thing breeds another, but that does not have to be a part of your life. Keep in mind that things are not near as bad as they appear.

Read today's scripture aloud several times.

Seek the Lord, for his guidance, leadership, and to hear a word from Him. Ask Him for guidance or for a word today. Say something like this, "**Lord I need to hear a word from you concerning…**"

_____

(Fill in the blank)

_____

_____

Zephaniah 2:3	**Seek ye the Lord…**

At the end of this special time with the Lord— **THANK Him** and **WRITE** all remarks, including what stands out during this aftermath. Remember to affix a date, time and place to your notes.

STAY IN THE RACE - HALFWAY THERE!

DAY 11—STAY FOCUSED

Don't veer to the left or to the right, keep your mind stayed on the right thing, no matter what comes up. Believe it or not, we are half way through this **GROWTH SPRINT**.

Keep your eyes on **Jesus Christ**. Don't compare yourself with another human. In the midst of turmoil and difficult times stay focused - don't look on the problem, as fate would have it magnified, larger than large. Trust me; when a person focuses on the problem or condition more than on what God can do; they will not find themselves growing, nor will they be able to spring forth. Have you heard of the phrase 'marking time'? In my words this means getting nowhere very fast or almost at a complete stand still.

Most people can think of a situation or catastrophe that can cause them to not see anything or anyone but that disaster. **TODAY** get such a situation in mind and **REBUKE IT**, say: "I will not **focus** on you today, I will leave you with **Jesus**—He will fix this. **Thank God** and **bless His name** and Don't mind at all if by now with up lifted hands that the Lord may move inside you a feeling that you have not felt before or a tear may fall, because **He is God**.

Read aloud the scripture several times.

Philippians 4:8	**Whatsoever things are lovely, think on them**

When it is time to leave or end this session with the Lord, and you will know; write down comments, thoughts, and things that come to mind that will make an impact on what happened today, as well as reading your daily entries months or years later. A lesson well-learned is to write at will by the auction of the God of Heaven.

Notes:

DAY 12 – Today you will meditate on the Lord.

You will be **READING a spirit led passage**. Ask Jesus to show you what to read. This is what might happen: you may then feel or sense a certain book and chapter, you may open the Bible and read what it opens to, or you may read something that you did not understand the time that you read it before. You may be led to find a chapter pertaining to something that maybe going on in your family or your own life. A scripture is included just in case.

Read the chapter, **meditate on it**. What is meditating? It is to think about or ponder over what you have read and what it means to you; reread, even recite, and listen for feedback from the Lord.

Be sure to ask the Lord to show you what He wants you to know about that particular reading. Avoid all distractions and noises at this time. Apply the process of **FOCUS** –staying in tune with the **WORD**.

As the **Spirit of the Lord** inside you begins to speak to you in your heart, you will be able to write what you are hearing.

II Corinthians 3:2 .... **Known and read of all men**

After this time is over with the Lord, **WRITE** the comments or any insight that is revealed to you. Revisit your notes through the day and keep them in a safe place. X-out #12 on the daily counter, page 52, unless you plan to repeat this activity.

Notes:

DAY 13 – Praises unto Him

This is a great day a wonderful time to just come before the Lord with **praise and thanksgiving**.

The task today is simply to **Praise the Lord**. Praise Him for everything that you can think of. Even *'Praise Him for His mighty acts'*, for just being God. When you run out of praises, start to thank Him for blessing you, keeping you and your family, and saving you. Between thanking and praising Jesus, can anyone run out of things to say? When you think you are through, just think about JESUS, 5 or 10 years ago where you were in life. I am guaranteed that you will have a jump start of praise and thanksgiving all over again. Praise is like the gift that keeps on giving, there is no end; it does not run out.

This day you are not asking the Lord for anything, just giving praises **unto Him**. READ and PRAISE HIM. Many times, all any of us need to do is to think of the danger that we could have been in while we were traveling or the praise that comes each time you see a hospital, prison, or fast-food place of business. If you are not sick, in chains and bound, and of course not hungry; I am not saying that those that are in these situations do not have something to praise the Lord for. If you or I were to talk with someone in each of the fore stated situations, they would still have something to thank and praise the Lord for because they are living and not dead, that speaks volume. Yes, **you have been blessed,** and no one has to remind you of that, SO! **Thank the Lord.**

Psalms 150 *Let everything that has breath praise the Lord.*

Write all images and visions that come to mind after this session is over. Keep good records and accounts of what the Lord is revealing to you during this **GROWTH SPRINT**.

Notes:

DAY 14 – Today Sing Unto the Lord a New Song

Sing? Yes!

I know your first thought is perhaps, I cannot recall any songs that the Lord may like. That is just the point. If no song comes to mind, then, make up one. If that does not happen, read one of the 150 Psalms located in the **Old Testament** of the Bible.

Made up songs are God inspired ones and the Lord can give you a song if you ask Him. When He gives you a song or better yet when he helps you to make up a song, be sure that you record it in your notes, word for word as much as possible. The best blessing is when you have been given the words of a song to sing, and you hear yourself sing a God inspired song with a tune. You are blessed and you will be a blessing to others.

Read the daily scripture and sing unto Him aloud.

Didn't Jesus make this day easy, and you were able to get through it with a **NEW SONG**.

Stay in the race! You are going down toward the finish line.

Psalms 33:1-3	*Sing unto the Lord a new song*

Write the song if it was made up or just write the title of the song that you did sing. If you made it up be sure that you write out the words even give it a title and something about the tune for it as well. You never know that song may be a hit song one day.

Notes:

DAY 15 – Have an Open Heart

This is an open day that you come before the Lord with whatever you choose or feel that you need to bring before the Him. It may be negative or positive, such as, I cannot get along with a person on the job or not able to get along with a family member, also Lord I need help with my bank account.

Your choice, you make the selection, and bring this concern to your special place today.

Also, you may have a project or something to complete; you can bring that before the Lord as well and get more insight or advice to help complete or accomplish the task.

I am a living witness that the Lord will help you in time of trouble. One day as I was praying, the Lord heard and answered my prayer; while I was still on my knees. Commit yourself to the Lord and His Word; you will see that the word of God gets busy working on your behalf.

Ask the Lord out of a sincere heart and believe He will answer you, He will help you, He will keep you, and He will protect you. What do you need the Lord to do?

Ask: "_____

_____?"

This day, for sure, you need to be a very **skillful listener that you may hear your answer.**

Hebrews 4:16   *Grace to help in time of need*

Write it. Exactly what your request was and what was given to you as you heard in your heart.

Notes:

DAY 16 – Special gifts and talents

Today it is important to bring any known gifts or talents in the presence of the Lord. Many of you may or may not have thought about the gifts or talents that you may possess. Whether it is singing, drawing, sewing, speaking, and that list can go on and on. However, I am sure that the Lord can and will reveal your gifts to you when you ask Him. Everyone has gifts, talents, or abilities inside them whether they have tapped into them or not. The one tactic that may be used against you to cause you to miss out on your gift coming forth is FEAR.

The Bible uses the term **spiritual gifts** not just gifts in the context of what is meant in this day. Those gifts are bestowed by the Holy Ghost to edify the church as you will see when you read and study the boxed scripture at the bottom of this page. There you will find a list of the spiritual gifts.

According to Webster's dictionary, gifts and talents are closely related that says a special ability without applying a mind of extraordinary power.

A way to gauge your abilities is to think about what it is that you really like to do, and it can be done with ease and no sweat. The gift flows freely.

Lay your gifts before the Lord, and **ask Him to reveal your spiritual gift** as well. Thank Him for your gifts and ask Him to help you to prefect them and use them to His honor and glory.

I Corinthians 12:1-11	*Now concerning spiritual gifts...*

Write any gifts from the list that you have a strong feeling for and any other ability that may come to you, that may not be on the list.

Notes:

DAY 17 – BIND UP FEAR

Fear is dangerous. It will cause one to miss out, loose out, be counted out, and sell out. **DO NOT ENTERTAIN FEAR for one minute. You must denounce it and trust the Lord.**

Fear having free range in your life will be more deadly than any germs, lurking in your body; it will stunt or even stop your growth.
Fear may come in many forms such as sweating, shyness, or uncertainty about something that you should have knowledge of.

The best catalyst to combat fear is to know the **WORD** and to believe the Lord. You cannot doubt the Lord; you must believe and keep moving in this race. Don't allow anything to stand in your way. To accomplish this is to not give way to any fearful thoughts or acts. You should stay focused; and continue to stand on the promise of God's Word. This negative spirit has not come from the Lord. Commit to studying and believing the Word. It does work!

Read aloud the scripture.

Today, **Ask the Lord to not allow any trace of Fear to come upon you** and to protect you. Also ask the Lord to show you what fear is like as it works inside of you and what is the best way to stay clear of the force of it; and how to defeat fear once and for all.

II Timothy 1:7 *For God has not given us the spirit of fear.*

Write your feelings and any comments or concerns that will help you to understand what God has done. What was revealed to you about how fear feels and how to recognize it? What to do to defeat the force of the spirit of fear? After this you should not be plagued with fear again. Halleluiah!

Notes:

DAY 18 – Without LOVE nothing will work

Love is the focal point of all things in life, without it you are nothing and have nothing. Today you will ask the Lord to show you how to be more loving and kind to others. You may start by asking yourself how do you see others, or can you see the good in others, and show me how to love even when someone may not be lovable. Biblically speaking, we are instructed to love one another as we love ourselves. In other words, love what you do, love yourself, love others and things pertaining to life. Love the Lord.

Always speak positive in your own life and in relationships that God is bringing to you, which will bring more love into the situation.

By now you know how to ask the Lord for what you need and want. It may go something like this: "Lord, show me how to love, Help me to overlook faults and short comings of others and to love instead. I believe your word, when it says "Love will hide a multitude of sins" cited in 1 Peter 4:8. You showed me that when you saved me, and filled me with your love, in Jesus name. Thank you Lord!

Eyes closed, hands lifted up, or bow down in the presence of the Lord as **He fills you and seals you with His LOVE. Halleluiah!**

Stay there to receive your in-filling of His love.

Aloud: read, ask, and receive.

I Corinthians 13   *Faith, hope, and love the greatest is charity*

Write all that happened, how you felt, and anything that is gain from this experience with the Lord today. Revisit your notes periodically.

Notes:

DAY 19 – PATIENCE

Many people have little or no patience. Just cannot sit, stand, wait, or even tolerate others well. This kind of temper may be very short like something boiling over. They have to have cooling off spells, from being or getting so mad or upset with someone or something. I am not speaking of any particular person, but I am sure you know someone just like that. Remember, the Lord knows you better than you know yourself. **He knows your patience**.

Do come before Him in humility, and if the above paragraph describes you or anyone; there is room for **PATIENCE** to come alive.

Patience is also listed in Galatians as a fruit of the Spirit; again if you do not have any patience then that Spirit is dormant inside of you. Be sure to read aloud the daily scripture.

Ask the Lord to wake up that Spirit inside you, and give you more patience, and teach you to enter into **His PEACE**. The opposite of patience is peace, and they are both part of the fruit of the Spirit that is mentioned in Galatians. You need grace from the Lord to stay in His presence; refuse to allow negative vices to ride in your life, seek help in overlooking the faults of others, and any other thing that may be given to help offset the stubborn spirit of No Patience.

After you ask the Lord, **wait for Him to do the work**. Speak it out of your mouth, that you will have patience when the Lord gets finished with you.

Hebrews 12:1-2	*.....run this race with patience*

Write all ideas, thoughts, and comments that you hear in your heart. Take care in capturing on paper what you have experienced.

Notes:

DAY 20 – "Endure unto the end"

(Today's reading) – It seems people do not have any problems getting started, but the task comes someplace between start and finish. You must feel great because you are still blazing in this **GROWTH SPRINT**, so hang in there for one more day. I am convinced that if any person can **HEAR** the Lord, they would not stop or come short of completing a task, because He is speaking and coaching along the way. Keep on going! No One Wins when they stop even if they are two steps from the **FINISH LINE.**

What is one of your greatest shortcomings? Give it to the Lord today. He will replace it with a greater quality. He is the One that can change any situation and set the outcome. **HE IS GOD**! Trust that He can, and He will do it for you. Believe God in your heart of hearts. **You have come too far to stop now,** not only with this Growth Sprint, but with what life has to offer. Stand tall, run a little longer, and keep your eyes on **the prize-Jesus-the Finish Line.**

Read aloud the daily scripture.

Ask The Lord to help you to **ENDURE:** unto the end in this race, your life, your endeavors, and in His Word. He will see you through because you know that He hears you. Going all the way until the end, is that inborn strength that everyone needs to complete a task. I am confident that the Lord will and can show you the way and how. **ASK and WAIT!**

Mark 13: 13 ......*Endure unto the End.*

Write down any comments, feelings, or words that come to you while you are in the presence of the Lord. (Not only what is heard for the moment, but any thoughts that may come throughout the day.)

Notes:

DAY 21 – TEACH ME TO WORSHIP YOU WITH JOY?

This is a time that you are asking the Lord to take you beyond thanksgiving and praise on into worship with a greater allegiance to Him. You are almost at the **FINISH LINE** and there is no better time to learn about **WORSHIP** than right now. Make sure that you are in a teachable mode, without any distractions.

The Bible says that the Joy of the Lord is my strength. To worship the Lord you need to have joy down in your soul. No one that is sad can come into the presence of God, and remain in that sad spirit; he will move from sadness or no joy, to having unspeakable joy. As joy comes upon you, you will be ushered into a greater dimension of praise/ **worship.** This is not your doing, but the doings of the Spirit that the Lord has placed inside you.

Read aloud the scripture.

Ask Him to give you that JOY and move you to a deeper level of praise / worship, **Wait** for Him to bless - **open your mouth** and **praise Him**, do not pay attention to what you are saying or doing just allow the Spirit to **worship the Lord** through you. Do not be confused if you hear a language that you have not heard before; this is worship unto the Lord, and He understands. This is the day that you recognize Him as Father and call Him, *"Abba Father"* as so revealed in His Word (Romans 8:15).

YOU SHOULD FEEL STRONGER and THANKFUL AFTER RECEIVING THIS GREAT JOY. I know you do not want to leave this place in His presence; it is very refreshing, and you feel soooo goood! Thank you, Lord for feeling me with great joy!

Nehemiah 8:10 ….; *for the joy of the Lord is my strength*.

Record in your notes the date, time, and place including all comments and any other expressions of adoration.

Notes:

21-DAY CHALLENGE COUNTER

Use this counter to help you keep track of the day. After each day cross out the number, then you will be ready for the next day without guessing or trying to remember the number of the last day.

1	2	3
4	5	6
7	8	9
10	11	12
13	14	15
16	17	18
19	20	21

Daily: Simply **X-out** any day that you have completed and do not plan to repeat.

Weekly: Simply **X-out** #1 after seven days, #2 after seven more days and proceed.

"TO BE WITH YOU" – God inspired song

I want to be in your presence.
I want to be in your presence.

I need you to lead me Lord.
I need you to guide me.

Without you I'll not make it.
Without you I'll be nothing.

My rejoice is in your Love.
My rejoice is in your Grace.

Just trust and obey.
Just believe and receive, yes!

I want to be with you.
I want to be in your presence.

Halleluiah, Halleluiah to the King of Glory and Praise.

The Author, *KMR*

THE CHALLENGE IS OVER; DON'T LET THIS BE THE LAST TIME THAT YOU TALK WITH THE LORD IN YOUR OWN SPECIAL PLACE AND TIME.

WHOLESOME GODLY RELATIONSHIP

You and Him

AFTERWORD

Don't miss your time with the Lord. When you first opened this book, you may not have been up to The Challenge, but since you were willing to help yourself, you took it on. In doing so, you were assured that it was something that you could do with a made up mind.

In this book, I talked about a special place and time to come before the Lord—**that was being in His presence**; no, you did not see Him, but when the experience was all over you knew that you had been in His presence. That time and place that you chose was for you to stay on point, be on time and prepared—God is ready. This message is all about Relationship, and a sincere desire to excel in Faith while being saved from yourself and the world.

The note-taking that you record daily from your experiences should be recorded in such a way that you would be positive and not doubtful in your heart that the Lord is real, He will deliver, and answer when you call on Him. On all of your notes you should have inscribed the date, time and even place, so when you revisit them you would know the reference of it or you could see the progress of your relationship with Jesus, the Lord.

Your choice of Bible to read for this experience was to give you the freedom to use the book that you were most familiar with. To have specified a Bible may have proposed a problem especially if one had been recommended, and you did not have it, or had to go out and purchase one. The best way anyone will get to know God is through **His WORD**, there is no way I could have written a book like this without having you to have a Bible on hand and physically look up the devotional chapters and read in repetition. The word cleanses and changes lives as **READING** is implemented.

I appreciate you for taking this challenge and being obedient to this message, but more importantly being obedient to the Holy Spirit. The mission of this book was to allow The Spirit to have His way. Mission accomplished! Make up in your mind to seek the Lord more, and do not try to live in this world without Him or His help.

Don't let this be the last time that you come into the presence of the Lord at a designated place and time. In the presence of the Lord there is everything that you need, including the fullness of joy and liberty according to the Bible, and now you can say that you are a living witness.

Through this book the Lord has shown **His GLORY** and all you did was stayed the course to the end, <u>followed his instructions</u>, and <u>met</u> <u>at the same place and same time.</u> **The rest was up to Him.**

As you are going through life, you see that you are not growing; and you find yourself doing the same things in the same way and place without any progress; you know you need HELP! Come back to this book as a starting point and find your way again.

Time is of essence and more important now than ever before. Days, weeks, months, and years are coming it seems faster than any other time in history. It is time to learn to seize the moments and opportunities that are set before you.

> Matthew 16:26 *"For what profit is it to a man if he gains the whole world, and loses his own soul? Or what will a man give in exchange for his soul."*

Pace is what most sprinters have to be conscious of in a race. If they are not careful, they will lose momentum and will miss the plan, which is TO WIN. Most people can say as they paced down the tracks of life that the way was unstable, not moving, nor growing. When you look around and find yourself behind as in the rear or back of everyone else; no one or nothing has to tell you to pick up the pace, because you can see it.

So look around you now and pick up the pace of life toward those things that really matter and will cause you to partake in the Kingdom of Heaven. Don't lag behind unless you are restoring energy and will be the first at the finish line.

The challenge is up to you, because you can do something about this Sprint of Growth in your life. Remember, no one can run this sprint for you, **YOU MUST DO IT**. You do not want to end up short of the **VICTORY**. Be an aggressive sprinter; your life depends on it as you travel through this world. Keep on treading! You will be aware of how you are doing and eventually you will be at the end.

Whether you live or die, there will come, an end to the Sprint of Life. Regardless of how you corn it: the end, all over, a looser, or no opportunity for another chance, it will be as Christ uttered from the cross, **"IT IS FINISHED"** *(St. John 19:30).*

I Corinthians 9:24-27   ***Do you know that those who run in a race all run, but only one gets the prize......................***

Will you finish and get the prize? **Only YOU can answer this request.**

I am confident that after this experience that you now see how important it is to have a real **relationship** with the Lord. And to know for yourself that He wants to <u>fellowship with you</u> more than you with Him.

This experience should help you to know God better, hear Him more effectively, and trust Him. Read your own writings over and over; don't stop going before the Lord just because this book has ended the challenge. <u>Now is the test for the real challenge in your life when problems arise and things are going wrong; what are you going to do?</u>

The <u>mission</u> was to <u>lead</u> you long enough and <u>wane</u> away from the experience in such a way that you will have the will power to continue going into the presence of the Lord. You know that nothing gets done successfully in life without the **HELP** of the God of Heaven. You may feel led to do another session of 21 days from this book, by all means take the challenge as much as possible to help you stay on task and focused on the things of **Righteousness.**

Another task was to help develop you in such a way that you would be a **witness** for the <u>kingdom of heaven,</u> as you share your experiences with others. When the Lord does something, you just cannot keep it to yourself, even when He tells you to tell no one. There are several accounts of '*go and tell no one*' in the Bible; read the given scripture; however, there are many others.

Matthew 9:27-31   ***"See that no one knows it."***

> Philippians 1:6 *"Being confident of this very thing that He who has begun a good work in you will complete it until the day of Jesus Christ."*

So continue:

Praying　　　　　　**Obeying**　　　　　　**Reading**

　　　　Meditating　　　　　　**Asking**

Writing　　　　　　**Believing**　　　　　　**Receiving**

　　　　Witnessing　　　　　　**Praising**

H A L L E L U H I A H!

H A L L E L U H I A H!!

H A L L E L U H I A H!!!

(This is the highest praise.)

ABOUT THE AUTHOR

She is the distinguished Katherine, first born of the late Linwood and Jessie who later divorced. Raised by her father and grandparents including four other siblings with help from other family members, she was a real go-getter, and would not allow anything or anyone hold her down.

She is an ordained minister of the gospel, and has held her own radio ministry, The Late Hour Message Ministry, as an evangelist on several stations. The list of some of her accomplishments are as follow: associate pastor at large church, lead intercessor on national prayer line, host her own television ministry, same name as radio ministry above, on local access station, taught: Bible School, Bible Study, Sunday School, pastured several ministries including Senior Ministry, Singles Ministry, outreach ministry, and now to include writing which is the latest platform that she has undertaken, and the list goes on. This is her first book of many more to come.

What will she do next? You have to ask her.

IT'S UP TO ME

Walking, running, moving across the terrain of life,
Determined not to be bitter or full of strife.
Treating each one I meet with love,
As the Lord keeps me as humble as a dove.

When I rest, I will not stop;
Just long enough to end on top.
I asked the Lord to help me today.
So I know I will make it come what may.

I asked, show me your glory and favor too.
And help today to do all I need to do.
Thank you Lord for hearing me,
'cause it is still up to me, I see.

I MUST ASK!

Author K. Mooring- Ruffin

YOUR PATH OF LIFE

This path can be straight, full of obstacles, or whatever you bring into it. I am persuaded that The Word of the Lord can be a light and a lamp to a dark path especially because the Bible says so in Psalms 119:105.

START   You

Everything done between
Start to finish is
Up to YOU!

FINISH LINE   **YOU**

*************AWARD'S DAY************

CHALLENGE

GROWTH SPRINT IN 21 DAYS

************* FIRST PLACE ************

BLUE RIBBON

*Sprinter*_____
                    Your Name

CERTIFICATE OF COMPLETION

This certificate is presented to:

_____

Name

For completing the Growth Sprint In 21 Days

_____

Date   *Time*   *Place*

_____

Your Signature   *Date*

_____

Witness (Holy Spirit)   *Date*

To be completed by you for you.

OTHER BOOKS   by Katherine Mooring-Ruffin

    ✓ **<u>BLESSINGS-FILLED POCKETS</u>** – an Inspirational Book

    ✓ **<u>A PULPIT COMES YOUR WAY</u>** – A Manual of Sermons

    ✓ **<u>THE 3rd PART OF THE TRINITY</u>** – to inform

If you are pleased and happy with this book, send one to a friend, and consider purchasing one of my other books.

Thanks,
Katherine Mooring-Ruffin

CONTACTING US IS EASY!

We would like to hear from you. Please send your comments about this book to the email address below. Thank You.

Email: ruffin_katherine@yahoo.com

Twitter: @kruffin09

YouTube

Facebook

www.ingramcontent.com/pod-product-compliance
Lightning Source LLC
Chambersburg PA
CBHW031612040426
42452CB00006B/491